Serendipity!

To Jon 2
May you prosper and be
in health, even as
your soul prospers!

Colleen B. Truly

Serendipity!

30 day devotional

Carla Rae Fawley

authorHOUSE®

AuthorHouse™
1663 Liberty Drive
Bloomington, IN 47403
www.authorhouse.com
Phone: 1-800-839-8640

© 2011 by Carla Rae Fawley. All rights reserved.

No part of this book may be reproduced, stored in a retrieval system, or transmitted by any means without the written permission of the author.

First published by AuthorHouse   09/07/2011

ISBN: 978-1-4634-2065-9 (sc)

Printed in the United States of America

Cover photo by Blake Fawley

This book is printed on acid-free paper.

Because of the dynamic nature of the Internet, any web addresses or links contained in this book may have changed since publication and may no longer be valid. The views expressed in this work are solely those of the author and do not necessarily reflect the views of the publisher, and the publisher hereby disclaims any responsibility for them.

Author's email address: carlaraefawley@gmail.com

I dedicate this book to my mother because she is dear.

Preface

I love stories! When I became a Christian I bought one of those children's story books, since there was so much to learn and it was easy reading as a new believer. Then I discovered the 700 club on tv and got hooked on the testimonial portion of the show . . . . my husband would walk in and find me with tears running down my face. We need to share more of our victories with each other . . . . we all need encouragement . . . . Though I can be unconventional it doesn't mean I'm a rebel against doing things proper. But when I attempted to have my book professionally edited, I felt stripped of my personality. It just didn't sound like . . . . me. Kind of like the time I was told to change my signature because it wasn't perfectly legible, I understood, but it was something very personal taken away. What your reading is a raw memoir from my heart . . . . I think you'll receive it just fine.

Foreword

I'm writing the forward to my wife's book because she asked me to, and because I know her best. Humorously speaking their is no doctrinal error to beware of it's just her life in a devotional format. She like so many women desires to use her mistakes, trials and triumphs to encourage others because like she says "were all going through stuff and it makes us feel better when we share it." Prayerfully consider her encounters and be blessed. Then go out and make your own story!

Steve Fawley
Vineyard Community Church - Syracuse, Indiana

Foreword

When I first met Carla she made me smile. She still makes me smile as life pours from her heart. I appreciate Carla's sincere faith and genuine love for others. Her kindness has welcomed me to this new place I call home and has showered me with tender loving care. I believe Carla has treasures of wisdom to be shared that are like jewels she has gathered along her journey of life in which we could all benefit from hearing.

Beth Callahan, wife of associate Pastor Sheldon Callahan
Vineyard Community Church

Day 1

. . . . just another dumb girl . . . .

. . . . I swallowed and took the correction because he was right. My brother was giving me advice that would stay with me forever. I was a teenager and just received salvation. He shared about character, and not following the crowd, backbone, commitment, and the Narrow Way. It hurt but I guess the truth does sometimes and besides I needed to face it . . . . I was just another dumb girl. Everything was new to me. He encouraged me to move to his house several hours away to get away from my friends that would drag me down. His church became mine, and I was surrounded with a group of youth like I've never seen or experienced before. It was all a culture shock. Never being around so many real Christians (outside Debbie Julians family and a few that said they were but you know . . . .) what a group of sweet sincere people! A few weeks later there was an opportunity for some of us to be baptized in the lake and my questions were answered on the purpose of why your entire body is laid in the water and raised up again. But there was just one problem . . . . their was going to be a pizza party fellowship with all my new friends, pizza, and cute boys, so . . . . I was thinking maybe there would be other opportunities to be baptized because I didn't want to miss the party. This was to be my first experience with the voice of the Holy Spirit speaking to me. It was almost like a person speaking . . . . only in my heart, and it scared me, yet, bringing home all the things my brother was trying to tell me. "IF YOU MAKE WRONG CHOICES NOW WHAT WILL YOUR LATTER END BE?" Something happened in the heavenlies that evening as I was raised from the water. Making my beginning steps, a series of right choices. Maybe not always perfect but it started a new pattern and little by little I was developing the character God was expecting.

day 1 . . . . What is one sin that is besetting you?
_____ Hebrews 12 :1 . . . . let us lay aside every weight, and the sin which easily besets us . . . .

> "Father help us to have the second chance we need to change . . . . and then another until we become all you want us to be . . . . In Jesus name."

Day 2

. . . . were standing right here . . . . we can hear you!

. . . . as we were browsing the department store, these two fellows walk by us . . . . one says . . . . "Man if that was me I'd kill myself" . . . . that was supposed to be funny because they both chuckled and walked away. I suppose we did look a little conspicuous . . . . me, the mom, 6 months pregnant following dad and son, with my 3 daughters . . . . all stair steps in age. It wasn't the first time we were the brunt of those kind of comments. In thinking of the guys comment, I don't think my husband was exactly suicidal. But truthfully it was a lot for a man when their is only one income especially with a large family. Somehow we always had everything we needed and more. Ironically just five or ten minutes later, a lady on the intercom spoke of a sale in the children's section.Quickly making it over to see what this sale included I found it was a whole rack of girls clothes 4,5,6. The very sizes of my three daughters! Looking at the bill as we walked out the doors I found we had purchased over three hundred dollars worth of clothes for thirty three dollars, and I soo wanted to chase down those fellows and brag how God loves us and takes care of us, but we just winked and smiled between the two of us, walking out into the parking lot happy and content.

. . . . day 2 . . . . In what area of your life do we need to take limitations off God?_____ Ephesians 3:20 . . . . unto him that is able to do exceeding abundantly above all that we ask or think . . . .

"Father cause us to prosper in ways above our normal income, in ways only you could work out! Surprise us! In Jesus name Amen!

Day 3

. . . . I don't need a brand new car to make me happy but I want to at least like the one I buy . . . .

. . . . in this situation their wasn't much of a choice. This car lot was the only one that would take our trade in, so we weren't leaving without making a choice. I know it was taking too long to decide but I just didn't feel settled. As we test drove yet another vehicle, my husband and I talked and shared about what we really desired, and the two that we narrowed down were close to what we wanted . . . . not perfect, but close. On the way back we prayed, not wanting to take second best. I hate to make a decision without peace, and never under pressure. We sat at the desk with 3 of the salesmen waiting for us to move forward, but we just couldn't without knowing for sure that it was Gods will. It was comical just sitting there waiting for the perfect vehicle to drop down from heaven, not wanting to leave but not wanting to commit. Then, up drives the exact car we wanted!! Color, size, everything! As I ran over to the window exclaiming "That's the one! "Does he work for you?" "Is it for sale?" They fumbled around a little, being caught off guard, but in the end shuffled the associate and all of his personal items out, cleaned it and gave it to us for a great price. The doubts and hesitancies left and peace took it's place. I've made enough mistakes and gotten to the place that I'm not interested in making a purchase without that serenity that abides when your moving in Gods will! We were excited driving home that evening. "I've seen some pretty wily car salesmen," my husband said, ... but that wasn't planned by them, God knew what we wanted and brought it to us."'

day 3 . . . . If your human like the rest of us, you have made mistakes from ignoring Gods spirit within. What have you learned and how can you change?_____

> "Father help us to forgive ourselves and discern not only our purchases but all our decisions that we would have that clarity to move ahead or the grace to hold back when we feel that hesitancy from you to wait. In Jesus name amen"

Day 4

.... "Isaiah 40:2 .... her warfare is accomplished" ....

.... thats the scripture that came to me upon awakening that morning. My bible was still open on my bed and having spent most of the night praying and pacing the floor .... I needed a word from the Lord! You know what it's like .... going through prolonged discouraging circumstances without any change, in spite of feeling like your doing everything you know to do. I'm not saying I was in despair .... my faith was still there .... I was was just tired ... and discouraged. It was like being in a very deep valley, all alone. The passage was speaking to me that this trial was coming to an end, ... But there was no time to think about it .... I had to be up and on my way. Later while clearing my lunch tray and throwing the wrappers in the trash . . . . I looked up and in that moment, everything around became dim and the picture on the wall came alive to me . . . . it was a beautiful mountain scene with a deep valley . . . . made to reveal at the very deepest point the most lush and fertile ground . . . filled with beautiful flowers and foliage . . . . it was the insight I needed . . . . and in the coming days and weeks, as I transitioned out of the valley I found it all to be true!

day 4 . . . . Do you have Gods mind about what your going through?_____ If not, don't ever be afraid to ask for wisdom! James 1:5- . . . . he gives generous wisdom, without reprimanding, ask in faith boldly . . . .

> "Father sustain us through our dark times and bring very beautiful things from it. In Jesus name!"

Day 5

. . . . unexpected commissioning

Remember when they used to cruise down main on Saturday night and groups of kids used to stand for hours talking and checking each other out? . . . . That was years ago before they put a stop to it . . . . Well our family was at the Deeper Life Conference one weekend, just walking distance away, and all the children were being entertained at the building across the road which happened to be a storefront with a full view of everything going on in the street. We took turns babysitting the kids through the weekend and when it was my turn I got put with Charlotte whom I had never met before. I immediately took a liking to her and was touched by her life story as we chatted. She expressed her desire to share with others and I told her how as teen girls we used to preach to people when we first got saved and told her it would be fun for her if she really cared about young people.

She agreed, and when we were relieved of our responsibilities, instead of going back to the seminar we stepped out into the street and proceeded to share about Jesus to everyone around. It was thrilling, and she fell right into a flow that was very mature . . . . afterwards . . . . at home that night I kept getting the feeling God was calling her to something in ministry and the scripture about sending forth his disciples kept coming to me. So the next morning, I sought her out at church because I knew it would be her last visit before going back to her hometown. I shared how I felt the Lord was commissioning her but it just didn't register and fell flat when I tried to tell her . . . . But a year later when our paths crossed again she told me how she had become the leader in a street witnessing program at a large church in New York City and how that first experience led her to her own ministry. I didn't know all that was going to happen but I did see a spark there that just needed a little encouragement. I'm not a minister . . . . I'm just a housewife, but I pulled out a fitting experience . . . . went with it and it grew from there . . . . now she has experiences that by far exceed anything I've ever done! That's how it should be . . . . with our children and with others . . . .

day 5 . . . . Are you aware of mentoring opportunities around you in your daily life? _____Who would benefit from a word in due season from you today?_____

"Father help us be ready for random and unexpected opportunities to mentor or encourage someone today, alert us to others needs and to be able to recognize their gifts so we can stir them to step out in it . . . . in Jesus name!! Amen!!"

Day 6

. . . . after the Dave Ramsey conference . . . .

. . . . so she tells me . . . . "God does not want us to be in debt, he wants us to be different, to be responsible, to owe no one but love. We're selling our Envoy and living within our means." What JOY! . . . . Then I had to take a road trip in the grandma car they bought. "Can you turn on the air conditioner its 90 degrees?" "Sorry mom just fresh air. You can do it mom." "Oh! What's that??! SPLAT! "Oh its just my drink, she says . . . . I forgot to take it off the roof before we left, I always set it up there when my hands are full because there are no cup holders." O well . . . . So as we're going down the road I plug my phone in because it's going dead." NO! Don't tell me, the lighter doesn't work!!! Are you kidding . . . . the radio doesn't work either? Okay fine . . . . I'll just use the last of the battery on my downloaded stuff . . . . Oh ya . . . . can't hear anything because we have to have all the windows open on the expressway . . . . because there is no air conditioning. If we make a stop for a drink on the way it won't be so bad. "Okay were almost there . . . . got our drink . . . . get the grandkids in . . . . " "Why is that man waving us down?" No, not because we're cute, it's because she forgot her drink again . . . . because there's no cup holders . . . . so we stop traffic a minute and we're on our way . . . . were pulling in the parking lot . . . "Ahh finally" . . . . so I begin trying to find a good place to throw a peach pit that would be respectable . . . . since peach pits are bio-degradable and not considered littering . . . . she says . . . "MOTHER DONT YOU DARE THROW THAT OUT MY WINDOW, WE ARE NOT HILLBILLIES!" . . . . She has since moved up a level and I don't have to ride in a clunker this summer. And all sarcasm aside I am proud that she sees it urgent to live a debt free life.

day 6 . . . . What does the Romans 13:8 principle mean to you?_____

> "Father help us in our finances to be pleasing to you, give us wisdom and help us to be the head and not the tail, a lender . . . . In Jesus name" Duet.28:1-

Day 7

.... every idle word ....

.... It was just one of many corrections that happened in the process of life. This incident happened after voicing my opinion about vitamins. Now .... it seems so stupid! But I was thoroughly convinced that taking a handful of supplements was baloney! "Its all in the mind .... why not just trust God!" But in time, and after having several children, I was found to be severely deficient in certain vitamins! To the point I couldn't function with normal strength. I tried very strict nutrient rich diets, juicing etc. but it just wasn't enough, I needed concentrated doses. Of course! The very thing I had said was dumb came upon me! So, after coming to myself, and after asking God to forgive me for my ignorance as well as arrogance, I proceeded to correct the problem by drinking a health drink that contained everything I needed. (I was still too stubborn to turn to pill form because I never wanted to be one of those health freak people.) That's when God allowed me to see how really judgmental I was! . . . . Now I am very vain, the type of girl that wouldn't go down to the mailbox without makeup or go to the store without my hair fixed . . . . and that particular brand of protein drink contained an ingredient that I was allergic to, and guess what? . . . . I broke out all over my face! I was mortified! It took a couple months to get it balanced out and to many people it wouldn't be that big of a deal, but to me it was a very sensitive area! So . . . . breaking off that last bit of stubbornness I became very sorry for my flippancy and began to be interested in the health wave. In time the allergic reaction went away and my health was restored. When I look back at the big picture of all the different dealings in my life, and how they are so fitting to my personality it reminds me of that scripture in Psalms 23 . . . . thy rod and staff they comfort me. Sometimes when I look at the ironic chastisements, I giggle at His humor and at other instances I still fear and shake a little . . . .

7. Can you think of an example of God returning a little just retribution in your life out of correction?_____.
This can be a very painful area, but comfort comes with scripture, Hebrews 12:12&13 . . . . lifting our hands and making straight our paths . . . .

"Father help us see your loving hand, help us find hope and a future, and to never be discouraged or turn away, but run to you in it all!" Daniel 9:9 . . . . mercy belongs to God though we've rebelled against him! Micah 7:8 discouraged or turn away, but run to you in " . . . . when I fall, I shall arise!

Day 8

.... the chair

.... I love Jesus, my husband, my children, my friends, Wal-Mart, thrift shops (my life is very small) .... and peace! I couldn't ask my husband for the $12.99 it would cost for a new chair (this was when you could feed your whole family .... all nine of us .... for the whole week for $100.00). I had already spent my grocery money and I was going to trust the LORD for a new lounger. That was my peace .... not the everlasting, stable divine peace that came with salvation. Not the everyday peace that came by trusting that God was in control no matter what drama happened that day. It was the personal private peace that happened between 2:00 and 3:00 everyday at nap time. The peace that I MADE happen or else I was grouchy. "Father, please give me a new lawn chair .... above my husbands paycheck just between you and me .... in Jesus' name . . . . AMEN." After all, I had been looking forward to nap time since breakfast. They were beginning to wake up and I needed to tend to the little ones, but once again I said a quick "thank you" just to remind him it was important to me and off again to chores. You would think I'd be ashamed to even bring a need like this up with all the people going to prison and dying for their faith even in our day. Or to think that revival and the presence of God was on the forefront of every devout women of God and I was praying for a lawn chair? It takes spiritual energy to make application to pray, believe and thank God for parking spaces, speaking life to that dying tree out front, favor with the neighbors etc . . . . When my time comes to suffer for Jesus in some way . . . . I'm sure I'll make it through some how, simply because I have been making it day to day now for 30 years. When the lady at the thrift shop I frequented asked me, "Can you use this lounge chair . . . . its new . . . . somebody just left it here and we don't take this type of furniture?" "FREE?" I asked. "Oh no charge, you come here often enough it will be free!"

    . . . . day 8 When God answers your prayers or when a previous answer comes to your memory begin to document them and see how often He really does answer you!!_____(let's make this line a little longer!)_____

_____

"Father sometimes our lives seem very insignificant but as we look to you, do miracles in our everyday life! In Jesus name!"

Day 9

. . . . Giants in the land . . . . Joshua 14:9 . . . . surely the land where your feet have trodden shall be your inheritance and your children's forever . . . .

. . . . so anyways . . . . I had worked through quite a bit of spiritual struggles by this time . . . . (learning Gods voice from that of the devil, legalistic tendencies, misunderstandings of Gods word etc.) . . . . and was beginning to see through some of the tactics of the dark side. I was gaining a little bit more confidence in spiritual warfare at this point in my life, and during this time . . . . my husband and I were driving down the road one day and while musing in my heart on these things . . . . something very supernatural happened . . . . kind of all of a sudden I had insight about my weaknesses and fears and how I had been robbed and taken advantage of because of timidity, and the VERY moment of this revelation, and of my immediate resolve to arise and stand up against lies and bondages . . . . A MONSTROUS ROAR shrieked through the air that left us wide eyed and shaken! The transmission went out right then and there! I knew exactly what was happening . . . . the truck died and my spirit soared. This was the first of many breakthroughs in various areas and very dramatic. Spiritual warfare is just that, its spiritual, and he was showing me every battle is worth fighting for the sake of freedom and the gaining of ground for us, and our loved ones . . . . Well my passive personality didn't change overnight but It definitely was a turning point. I'm still working on being offensive but I definitely stopped being pushed around and stepped on by the devil . . . . it had to stop somewhere and that was my stake in the ground!

. . . . Prophetically speaking . . . . that place on the road where my truck died . . . . (the very exact spot!!!) . . . . I was yet to find out years later would be our first, and last home, and property we ever owned where we would spend many happy days in prosperity with our children and grandchildren . . . .

day 9 . . . . Do you feel you understand your personal warfare? Do you need to be more aggressive? What spiritual principle would help, to put in practice . . . . prayer of agreement (Math. 18:19), proclaiming a promise, worship warfare etc._____

> "Father give us wisdom about how to deal with our struggles, help us get to the root source!"

Day 10

. . . . you didn't do anything wrong, but I should have asked more questions . . . .

"Go ahead that's fine . . . . have fun!!" I was busy with company . . . . and didn't check out who the driver was. Later . . . . while rushing to the scene of the accident . . . . I found . . . . that deep place where you're connecting with God in the middle of chaos . . . . the place of truth . . . . and answers to hard questions . . . . and found peace . . . . even though my whole body was shaking. If I knew who the driver was going to be that night I wouldn't have let him go . . . . he was inexperienced and this was his second accident and a very serious one. The car was in a field after rolling several times. Even though it was on its side, the boys were able to crawl out and were all okay. The oncoming SUV was never hit, but still dealing with being able to move on because of fear and panic. The fire truck and ambulance were there but in the end . . . . everyone was going to be alright. Weakened and lying down in the back seat as we drove home he was wondering why and for what spiritual significance did this all happen. A shooting star suddenly ripped through the night in front of us, strangely falling straight downward . . . . simultaneously while answering . . . . no son, you didn't do anything wrong . . . . it was a snare, and the devil found nothing in you.

Day10 . . . . are you aware of why certain things are or have happened to you? Is it a trial of your faith? Correction? A snare from the devil?_____ "Father show us what conditions we need to meet to be found without hindrance to your power, in helping and delivering us from every trap. In the name of Jesus"

Day 11

.... A spiritual hug is something divine just to let you know everything will be okay .... eventually

.... I knew it was condemnation .... I just didn't know how to get free from it. I needed spiritual wisdom. Going to the evening service with purpose, I took the bread and juice as a symbol of all Jesus has done for me. I was full aware of his death and the freedom it gave me. I came away feeling the same but I was using faith at this point that he was going to help me. Being the last one up that night and as I was turning out the lights I was thanking him and reminding him when suddenly I was touched .... completely stricken by God's power. It hovered a long time that night .... a wonder not easily forgotten. It was a spiritual hug. Things didn't change right away because what I was going through wasn't something that could be cast out. It dealt with mind sets and wrong thinking patterns . . . . so it took time. He was just letting me know it was going to be okay . . . . eventually, ... and in the days, weeks, and months to come it really was!

day 11 . . . . Do you feel God is speaking to you? Are you receiving encouragement from the word? Isaiah 50:10- . . . . who fears the Lord and obeys . . . . walking in darkness with no light . . . . let him trust in the Lord and stay upon his God! Can you tell the difference between conviction and condemnation?_____

> "Father, though we may be in the middle of struggle and hardship, comfort and give us a peace that surpasses understanding, and bring us successfully through. In Jesus name"

Day 12

. . . . Sounds kind of funny to say my son ran away from home when he was 19 . . . .

. . . . however, it wasn't funny when we found the note on the kitchen table saying he loved us but didn't want to live to our standards. Wow! I felt stupid after thinking about it. I didn't see it coming, I can be very naive. I remember those nights at three in the morning just struggling with all the different emotions. What did I do wrong? Why didn't I notice the red flags? Question after question began to fill my mind when suddenly one very important attitude appeared. I was thinking back on my judgmental response toward parents of prodigals. I felt bad and still do. I'm sorry if I've ever judged you in that way . . . . I know bad parents can make bad kids but for the most part the christian dads and moms I know are trying their best to live the light they have. Learning and growing from mistakes, and trying to do better. Once I struggled through the different feelings, wrong and right, I found hope within the situation. As I dealt with these attitudes and shortcomings, and struggled with how to trust God and find peace, then it was a few short years before he was raising his family in the way of the Lord . . . . right next door from the very home he ran away from . . . .

> day 12 . . . . Are you puzzled by the choices of children or even other loved ones? Is there a loved one you need to commit to God in faith? _____He doesn't want you to be tormented by it.

>> . . . "Father, forgive us for our sins, help us raise our children, alert us to things were not seeing, don't let our children fall from your grace. Save our entire family, that all may enter heaven! Acts 16:31 In Jesus name!"

Day 13

. . . . so that's what a vision is . . . .

. . . . it was like a dream . . . . in front of me . . . . only I was wide awake!

What happened was . . . . my husband had built this beautiful custom-made mantle for a couple, and we were delivering it. It took a lot of effort once we got it in the trailer to tie it down then drive it very slowly and carefully making sure it didn't get dented or scratched on the way to the next town over to where he would install it. It was so heavy and at least a 2 man job but no one else was available . . . . so we both gave it all we had to get it there without getting it damaged. The house was low of a hill so we struggled down lots of steps then onto the porch . . . . we did it! . . . . Now get the key . . . . NO!!! Don't tell me!!! . . . . Its not there!! They must have forgotten and we were so discouraged! We walked around the yard praying and thinking what to do . . . . I honestly didn't think I had the physical strength to lift it back on the trailer and bring it back home . . . . as I closed my eyes and just waited for wisdom . . . . suddenly I saw it . . . . a person sticking the magnetic key box to the soffit of his house then walking away before it took ahold, then I saw it falling straight to the ground. Well the excitement took over and I ran over to the corner of the roof where the key should be . . . . it was rejuvenating! I knew it would be there! I looked straight down to the ground, swiped away the leaves and there under the debris was the little box with the key inside! What encouragement! I have lost a lot of keys since then and never had any supernatural recovery but that will always be a sweet memory! . . . .

day13 . . . . it's not weird to ask for visions and dreams . . . . acts 2:17 ask! Share a dream or vision you've had!_____

> "Father though today may be a mundane day with normal activities we believe you are working behind the scenes . . . . give wisdom naturally and supernaturally . . . . in Jesus name amen!"

Day 14

. . . . I guess saying I love all the time doesn't make it so . . . .

. . . . I had been a little grouchy . . . . a little moody . . . . but I had reason to be . . . . didn't I?

I remember exactly where I was standing the day God stopped me in my tracks and thrust me into a three day, intense journey of self examination after speaking two terrifying words to me . . . "YOUR DECEIVED!" That's all that was spoken to me by the Holy Spirit and I was left to figure out why. Now you would mock me and say "That's not too hard to figure out!" but I was immature newly saved, newly married and clueless! Those two words got my attention! I'm still embarrassed how self-absorbed I was . . . . not usually saying a lot on the outside but inside churning and fussing.

I just couldn't understand my husband . . . . if he really loved me he would . . . . I'm deceived?? What does that mean? It shocked me and scared me. My life stopped . . . . I did what I had to do . . . . but spent the next three days praying,searching,seeking reading my bible . . . . what was I doing wrong? (Don't laugh . . . . it wasn't funny at the time!) I went over my very simple life . . . . I took care of the kids . . . . kept up the wash . . . . (my husband could take care of himself . . . . I was busy!) I made the kids meals and fed him at dinner. When he left for work in the morning I was tired . . . . he could make his own breakfast! Why did he have to work all the time? I knew we were supposed to . . . . do all things without murmuring and complaining . . . . but did it count if it was just in your heart? When I thought of somebody deceived . . . . it would be like people that lived in a commune or a guy that had 5 wives! Why would God say that to me? I analyzed my life and it was beginning to dawn on me . . . . slowly I was seeing my attitudes . . . . no it was bigger than that . . . it was a mind set and God jolted me into looking at it! I was the one that was found lacking in love! So . . . . years later I still dote over my husband making sure I'm supporting him . . . greeting him at the end of a hard days work, making our home a place of peace,where he's respected . . . . I'm very secure in his love because he's proven it over the years. If I never tell him again how much I love him it wouldn't matter because its obvious!

day14.... introspection is good, it keeps us balanced! Can you relate to my story in any way?_____
Corinthians 13:5

"Father in Jesus name, please help us to be real in our love not just talk!"

Day 15

. . . so I was curious one day . . . .

. . . . and wondered what the exact date was I asked Jesus in my heart. I didn't need to know . . . . I just wondered. I thought back to 1977 and remembered it was around Easter, one day before the Good Friday service. Not having a computer and not even knowing what Google was, I figured it would be nice to research it at the library sometime . . . . since Easter falls on a different date every year . . . . Later my daughter and I dropped by the budget shop and she got into the nickel bin and found a stack of little notebooks. "Sure you can get those" I said, "they'll be great for practicing your name!" Realizing later when she brought one to me to show off her writing skills, I discovered they weren't really notebooks at all. They were little old calendars and the one she held in front of me was the year 1977!

day15 . . . . do you have moments of intimacy you've had with God that were really between you and him, little things, that wouldn't mean a whole lot to others but something very special to you? _____
Draw from those times, it helps get you through the times you don't feel him at all, it's like a kiss.

> "Father in Jesus name, give us special little divine touches to encourage and bring joy to our hearts all the days of our lives" Gen.48:15b

Day 16

. . . . people that have inspired me . . . . the Stutzman's . . . . kindness is contagious . . . .

. . . . So it was probably a little intrusive but I was desperate. It was a terrible day at work and I just needed to be around people that were nice, so I asked if I could tag along. What a sweet couple they were . . . . with 3 children a few years older than me. I so badly wanted to have a family myself. It was a very lonely time . . . . We went to the mall, walked around and ate. They were so refreshing to be with and I felt like a starving young women in desperate need of fellowship, and was received heartily! I would probably say they don't even remember encouraging me back then, because they were nice to everyone, noticing that their friendships included the very lowly and weak, yet also well respected church leaders. Not long after, I met my husband, got married and started having my own little ones. I soon lost touch with that precious family but found myself also sensitive to the needs of single lonely young people. Some came with my husband at lunch and sometimes we just adopted singles that were in our lives for a meal or a get together. Remembering the times when I felt desolate and just a word or a phrase would get me through the week. Years later my husband happened to be working with the man of this sweet couple and decided to bring our families together for a cookout and we reacquainted ourselves with them. Who would have known my daughter would end up marrying one of their sons!

. . . . day16 . . . . watch for signs of Gods sovereignty in your life! . . . . they are everywhere! Psalms 37:23 . . . "the steps of a good man are ordered by the Lord, and he delights in his way". What is a time that you know your steps were obviously guided by God?_____

"Father in Jesus Name, Their are so many hurting people, who do you want us to speak to today?

Day 17

. . . . Whew, ... I didn't think it was going to take so long . . . . Psalm 105:19 . . . . the word of the lord tried him . . . .

Cameron Dean . . . . (my youngest) means crooked nose . . . . but his nose isn't really crooked . . . . it was a family name and even though we named his siblings very carefully with meaning . . . . his didn't really mean much at all . . . . but . . . . he was called to ministry . . . . A little before he was born the Lord showed both of us he had a calling and then when he was six . . . . Cam confirmed it! . . . . He was so cute! That morning everyone was rushing around getting ready for school and Cameron was looking for his book bag and then . . . . just as if he suddenly remembered . . . . stopped . . . grabbed my hands and said "Mom . . . . God spoke to me last night!" I asked him what he said and if he was awake or if it was a dream and he said he was awake and God told him in his ear that he was going to preach all over the world and in jails . . . . then he picked up his bag and walked to school . . . . Well he did commit to the Lord at a young age but in the years that followed he didn't prove to be deeply spiritual at all . . . . then when he was 16 his life took a very dramatic shift . . . . not brought about by human effort . . . . and that is where he is at today . . . . broken for the lost, sensitive, mindful of integrity, and inward purity . . . . So . . . . the kid that confessed to smoking pot in 8th grade and getting drunk on cheap vodka in tenth grade, the kid that was so cocky in basketball and barely even graduated . . . . calls me as he begins his college classes, and says "Mom I lied today . . . . (so Im waiting for the other shoe to drop) . . . . I called the Homework Helpline for only high school students and I told them I was a senior . . . . (I started laughing!!!! . . . . I couldn't help it!!!) . . . but I called back and told them the truth" . . . .

day 17 . . . . do you feel God has promised you something that hasn't happened yet? _____John 13:9 If God really showed you, then it really will, wait for it!

> "Father bring to pass all the things you have whispered to us in the night . . . . help us to walk in your perfect path and timing and bring

forth the promises and the fullness of what our calling in life is and for the lives of our children . . . . in Jesus name . . . . AMEN!"

Day 18

. . . . for women only . . . . cuz we like to talk about feelings . . . .

My little toddler Blake was my little friend and companion the weekend a bunch of us girls went to the women's conference. My husband had his hands full with the other children and I thought I would bring little Blakey along. It was just our own church that weekend and the women in charge said she was thinking of asking me to share a little bit . . . . but ended up asking someone else . . . . my feelings were hurt a little . . . . I suppose . . . . anybody would feel a little overlooked . . . . kind of felt unimportant but I would never say so . . . . it took a little while to shake off self pity. That stuff is poison so I determined to have a nice time!! Anyway . . . . I was real careful that my boy was very quiet and didn't bother my friends because this was their time to be without children and be with other woman so . . . . we cuddled together and I had little toys and treats and during the break I let him run in the halls and at night he was so cute and slept through the night . . . . it ended up being so enjoyable to be with my friends and him too!! I still remember some of the things shared by the ladies even after all these years . . . . and when I dropped Dana off . . . . she paused before leaving and sincerely expressed how she felt touched by my loving relationship with my son . . . . well, it was such a sweet encouragement to me that day, and lifted my spirits . . . . kinda like I had something to share after all . . . .

> day 18 . . . . Do you know that others are watching you all the time? Do you know that demonstration is far more powerful than words? How can you demonstrate Gods love today?_____

> > "Father . . . help us to be content and secure with whatever light you give us to shine and give us those special opportunities just for us. Use us today in big and in small ways.In Jesus name"

Day 19

. . . . we really had a lot of fun the 2 years we roomed together . . . .

. . . . even though my old roommate and I have gotten busy with our own families, and drifted apart we still have such funny crazy memories. One of the sweetest is when we went to the fair and drove the "carnies" crazy . . . . we didn't mean to . . . . we were newly saved and wanted to tell everyone . . . . so every night of the Kosciusko County fair that summer we walked around telling everyone about Jesus and how they were going to hell! Well this was before they had rules about preaching on the fair grounds and mostly people were nice but the carnival men despised us . . . . you know . . . . the ones that set up their trailers on the dark side . . . . the smokey loud side, where we now tell our own children to stay away from because they have snake tattoos and smoke weed. Well . . . . we just barraged them each night . . . . and on the last day we brought bundles of homemade cookies and handed them to each person that gave us heck about preaching to them. I'll not forget some of the facial expressions . . . . shame, guilt, and even a little conviction. Some very hard faces softened when we told them we were there because we cared about them not because we wanted to make them mad. One particular hard fellow (even after treating us terrible all week) had tears in his eyes and confessed he was a backslider. I'm not saying everything we did was mature but where we were at, and at that time, it did touch a few including myself!

day 19 . . . . did you know that you don't have to be a minister to share with others? Did you know God wants to use us even if we feel inferior and weak? What is in your heart, that is very real to you, that you've learned about God, something you would love to share?_____

> "Father meet us where we are at, and use us in spite of our weakness's or lack of maturity . . . . grow and make us stronger and stronger . . . . in Jesus name amen!" Job 17:9

Day 20

.... the blizzard and the Angels ....

.... It's scary driving in deep snow, especially when its dark and gloomy and now was getting to blizzard conditions! I was tense with all the fussing and questions from the back seat. I think the kids were nervous too. We were out of our comfort zone and Dad wasn't with us to make us all feel secure with his common sense driving skills. Now what was I supposed to do if I start to slide? .... um .... slam on the brakes or not slam on the brakes .... I felt bad that I put my family in this position, but I knew if I started kicking myself my confidence would drag down and I needed to be strong. I turned the radio on and tried to keep the atmosphere light. Till the news came on .... warning everyone to stay off the toll road because of a white out and low visibility. They were predicting pileups. Kids lets pray! They weren't unfamiliar to praying for others but they asked innocent questions like . . . "Whats a white out?" "Are we gonna crash?" "Do we know them?" I told them that we may never know anybody involved or ever hear that our prayers did any good but that there are children that are afraid and there are daddy's just like theirs that needed help so they didn't get in an accident. So we all prayed together asking that God would send his angels to deliver the drivers and to keep them from fear and prevent pileups. That Sunday we were all wide-eyed when a man stood up and declared how God aided him and his daughter on the toll road during a white out that week and proceeded to give a dramatic account of how his car went air borne missing the other vehicles landing on the ground without being hurt . . . . thoroughly convinced of divine intervention, exclaiming . . . . "I just know God sent his angels for me!"

> . . . . day 20 . . . . Who is someone you desire to pray for, even out of your own personal need and weakness?_____ "Father, Help us to take our eyes off our own troubles and remember others and honor our prayers by doing miracles! in Jesus name amen!"

Day 21

. . . . humility is very beautiful . . . .

. . . . probably most examples of humility I've seen over the years would be just simple everyday people . . . . like the time Mr. Roe kindly apologized and helped his customer carry her packages out to her car, ... right after she berated him in front of everyone in his butcher shop (something like her bacon not being lean!) . . . . what a godly reaction he had . . . . Or Susy L. quietly praying for me under her breath while I embarrassed myself to another, then sweetly correcting me in private. Or the time at breakfast, It didn't seem to cross Kathy's mind . . . . the entire meal talking about my self and never even asked her how she was doing. Then their was Susan Campbell . . . . seeing my lack, and helping me be a better cook, and housekeeper, never my superior but as a friend. Or . . . . (Im so embarrassed) the time I purposely grabbed the seat next to the guest speaker and his wife . . . . while Ruthy took the one farther away so I could have a chance to hear and speak easily at the table. I've heard and read a lot about humility, and grasped that it is the beauty of holiness . . . . but what brings it home is all the lovely examples that paint a picture for me. I often wondered how humility can come so instantly and spontaneously to someone when put suddenly under pressure, I don't have it all figured out yet but I'm learning . . . .

> "Father give insight into what humility is all about, help us to become just that, not by human effort and self abasement but by your spirit of holiness . . . . in Jesus name!"

day 21 . . . . what area of pride . . . . like self-righteousness or superiority or all the many forms of it do you need help in? Don't be afraid . . . . admitting the problem is half the battle!_____

Day 22

. . . . talking and walking . . . . watching and praying . . . .

. . . . The crime rate was up in our little town and it was a matter of prayer as I walked a new route that morning. I prayed " LORD that you would make this town a safe place to live and that you would expose evil." I watch people's houses any way while they are gone for the winter so I try to stay alert checking freezers, leaks, heating and other necessities. I prayed that our town would . . . . "be like the land of Goshen . . . . protected by God." A couple weeks later I came across a suspicious vehicle and followed them a little bit in my truck . . . . getting their license number I gave it to the police. The car was stopped and searched and filled with valuables including 4 TV's! It was all very exciting especially because they robbed 4 of those very homes I had been strolling by just days earlier!!! "AMEN!"

> "We believe Father as we utter inspired words you are doing something in the heavenlies, in Jesus name"

day 22 . . . . what is an area that you would not only like to spend more time praying for but really do care about and want to see changed?_____

Day 23

. . . . I think it was insecurity . . . .

. . . . We were out with Eric and LuAnn that evening and we were walking ahead of the men talking and sharing together when I began to justify a certain action I had taken (it was something dumb that wasn't even sinning) and she stopped me gently with a wave of her hand and told me to forget it. I didn't owe her any explanation . . . . that she trusted in me and to relax! She wasn't going to judge me. Do you know how that made me feel? I did relax . . . . I felt at peace and my shoulders dropped. I felt God's heart in that. Later she brought me a "saying" that I made into a plaque which is still on my wall. The author isn't known so I can't give them credit but it's called "Ideal friendship". "Oh the comfort, the inexpressible comfort of feeling safe with a person. Having neither to weigh thoughts or measure words but pouring them all right out . . . . just as they are . . . . chaff and grain together . . . . certain that a faithful hand will take and sift them . . . . keep what is worth keeping and with the breath of kindness blow the rest away."

"My husband shared with me once after I was feeling rejected that not everyone in this life was going to like me . . . . and I've accepted that . . . . But I'm holding dear the ones that do! day23 . . . . do you have friends that are "safe" people to be around? Are you a safe person for your friends to confide in?

> "Father inspire each of us to love one another deeply, sincerely and freely in Jesus' name . . . . AMEN!"

Day 24

. . . . little by little . . . . Deuteronomy 7:

. . . . I had been praying about areas in my life that bothered me, places that weren't growing, or changing, so . . . . thinking fasting would help I started a schedule that fit my life and worked it around my family. I made a commitment to stay focused till a difference was made. At first it was hard but in time and consistency I started seeing some changes. The bible and the Holy Spirit seemed to come more alive to me and it started to encourage me. Little by little I was coming out of these dark places that were a hindrance from really living my life to the fullest. (Being embarrassed to tell my weakness I'll just give an example . . . . like deep water. Like a person that is afraid, and just avoids swimming their whole life . . . . who wants to live like that?!) But I think we all do in some way. I would read about Joshua and Caleb and be inspired to conquer giants instead of side-stepping them all the time. You'd probably think some of my struggles were dumb, but they were real to me. Just like your struggles are real to you . . . . So anyway during this time we happened to go on a family vacation down south. Inspired, while standing in front of my husbands camera, on a mountain top looking down into the valley below, I got a little dramatic and opened my mouth, lifted my arms and boldly proclaimed . . . . Deuteronomy.33:29 "my enemies shall be found liars and I will tread upon high places!" suddenly a tree behind me shook, and crackled, and fell with a thud to the ground! Now . . . . I know what the botanists say . . . . but Immediately my heart swelled with joy realizing what really happened!

day 24 . . . . are you growing in the Lord? Do you have specific fear or weakness that you need freedom from? If you could just focus on 1 thing what would that be?_____

> "Father, Help us to possess territory we've never known before, help us to be everything you called us to be! Free indeed! In Jesus Name! Amen"

Day 25

. . . . a little birdie told me . . . .

. . . . I was hanging out with people that were dragging me down . . . . they weren't pot smokers or shoplifters . . . . they were Christians with a forked tongue and I wasn't seeing it . . . . I mean I didn't want to see it . . . . being newly born again I was so naive (I still kind of am but learned a lot about discretion the hard way) . . . . "Do you really think you should be going over there?" my roommate warned . . . . as I walked out the door and down the street . . . . (I just brushed it off) . . . . as I got closer I began to feel more hesitant more unsettled within . . . . but i was just learning about being sensitive to the Holy Spirit . . . . soooooooo . . . . A BIRD POOPED ON ME!!! Over my head on my shirt and what was ironic was I had just read that scripture a couple days before . . . . Ecclesiastes 10:20 "Do not revile the king even in your thoughts or curse the rich in your bedroom, because a bird in the sky may carry your words, and a bird on the wing may report what you say"(realizing that is where we probably derived that saying you know about the bird) . . . . it was somewhat humorous but yet it wasn't . . . . God was trying to get my attention in a way I would never forget . . . . and I never did . . . . He further confirmed it as I was falling asleep that night . . . . I had already apologized to my roommate and settled it in my heart that I would be more careful to hangout with those that were positive and weren't so quick to be critical and gossip . . . . then He AUDIBLY whispered in my ear "John 17:21" Well!!! I didn't know how many chapters there were in John but I sure got up and read the passage ("John 17:21 . . . . I would that you all be one, even as I and the father are one . . . . ") and in that moment the big picture became clear . . . . that incident gave me fear, and direction that still guides me today . . . . we try not to backfire or gossip in our home. I'm sure I slipped many times over the years but my goal in life is to help and edify the church . . . . any church . . . . and to never speak evil.

> day25 . . . . do you feel you are avoiding unhealthy relationships as you should? Are you a positive influence?

"Father in Jesus name, you hear us even in secret places help us to examine what comes from our mouths,"

Day 26

. . . . I was dying . . . . or so it seemed like it to me! . . . .

. . . . atmosphere is everything . . . . so if I act miserable then it will dampen everyone's fun so I went along and made the best of it. Saturday afternoon in the city was hectic and the children and I were getting hungry. I needed to do my best to be pleasant because if I started getting annoyed and grouchy it would spread to the others. I always wanted our family to have that aura of peace and a unity between my husband and I but I was beginning to feel worse and worse . . . . it was a mixture of pregnancy and blood sugar problems. When he said, "why don't I drop you off and you can get the children and yourself something to eat?" I felt weak and my head was spinning. I needed protein, yet looking at the lines all the way to the door my heart sank.

But then in a moment (sensing we are no less than Joshua in this life) something very spiritual happened . . . . nobody noticed it, ... as I swallowed and in weakness stepped forward by a gift not of my own, I found my self walking to the front of the line. The people all in sync moved from side to side (Im very serious . . . . it was a mini red sea experience) and out flowed a new cashier ready to take my order . . .

day26 . . . . write down an instance where God delivered you or answered your prayer in a supernatural way_____

> "Father we are just regular people with regular problems, please meet us where we are at in supernatural ways, open our eyes though it may be hidden from others, in Jesus name!"

Day 27

. . . . so I asked God . . . . what does this mean . . . .

. . . . I'm confused . . . . hmm . . . . Proverbs 26:4 states "Answer not a fool according to his folly" . . . . and then Proverbs 26:5 says "Answer a fool according to his folly" . . . . give me wisdom Lord because that doesn't make sense! "The scriptures were new to me. Once saved, I devoured the Word, and wanted to know everything about the scriptures! . . . . So anyway it was a few days later . . . . I was pouring coffee for a drunk backslidden minister that happened to flounce into my designated booth . . . . I kind of put up with him, and had kept very quiet. It would have been stupid to feed his arrogance by conversing with him. He was brash,and boisterous, so the best of wisdom was to keep my distance as much as possible, avoiding getting sucked into his ridiculous conversation. But after his meal, he tried to hustle me and at that point . . . . having to consider my self-respect . . . . I firmly replied, "The Bible says not to answer a fool according to his folly." Walking away I had to giggle when I realized the LORD had just answered my prayer.

day 27 . . . . do you have questions about Gods word you don't understand?_____ask him! He wrote the scripture by the Holy Spirit!

> "Father give us divine demonstrations of your word, show us secrets . . . . in Jesus name!"

Day 28

.... yes I do have flashbacks .... several times a year

.... and that morning a whole cluster of memories came back to me.

I had just been thinking of all the narrow escapes from harm and accident. It was over several years time, but each instance that floated through my mind gave me a kind of shiver of fear of what could have happened .... the semi that almost smashed into us, the time Jared poked his eye with a stick, when Jaxon fell in the pond, losing little Carlena in the mall, and I knew if I thought for awhile their would be many other incidents. It all made me so thankful and my prayers were fervently asking for God to continue to deliver and protect in spite of our frailties. Afterwards I began my day with the huge project of cleaning my husbands work truck. He was gone and I wanted to surprise him, so I cleaned it all out, organizing everything real nice, all the stuff under and behind the seats, tape measures and screw drivers, and 5 coffee cups. He was going to be so surprised! It was a good truck and it was payed for . . . . a guy needs to be proud of his truck! It took a while but I got it shining and then off to the gas station to fill it up. As I pulled in and parked this guy kept staring at me . . . . now he was glaring! Well, I just ignored him and put my debit card in at the pump and picked the nozzle up . . . . O brother now he's coming over to me . . . whats his problem? "Excuse me" he said "Isn't that a diesel?" My breath left me and my knees were weak . . . this vehicle had no guard on it to keep the regular gas from flowing into it and if it had it would have ruined the motor! I still cringe when I think of that close call "Thank You Jesus! Yes! Thank You AGAIN!"

> day28 . . . . what are a few areas that God has delivered you?_____ it will build your faith to remember them! 1Samuel 30:6 . . . . David encouraged himself in the lord . . . .

Day 29

. . . . the washer woman

. . . . "Please don't wash this in the machine, it's my favorite . . . . it will shrink and it was very expensive!" I forgot . . . . AND IT SHRUNK! We had been married a few years and I always felt insecure about being a housewife. I so badly wanted to be like Mrs. Cleaver but my ignorance showed in my cooking, cleaning, and pretty much everything else. He never seemed to notice much. But I was really sensitive and today I totally blew it! How am I going to tell him? How am I going to redeem myself? I could throw it out and hope he never notices . . . . put it in the mending pile where things stay for years . . . . NO! I'm going to go straight out to the driveway and spit it out as soon as he comes home!!! I failed him again. I'm going to face it!!! I'm going to be honest about my mistakes! All day I felt doomed, it was easier if he would just yell at me but to look at his disappointment . . . . ugh. It hung over me all day (the negative seems SO big when we dwell on it . . . . weakness and besetting sins or things that aren't sins at all!) His truck finally appeared and I marched out to meet him bravely . . . . as a martyr . . . . someone about to be burned at the stake. It took courage and I spilled it out without crying and he responded with tears in his own eyes. Then, catching me off guard, he hugged me and said, "I ran into _____ today and the _____ are getting divorced. Who cares about that sweater, I'm just glad my wife loves me!" That incident helped me . . . . I felt free to be myself. I felt more secure when he told me he wanted companionship and support. He said, "If he wanted a housekeeper he would hire one!" Hmmmm . . . . maybe he will!!!!

day29 . . . . is there an area that your very insecure about, and causes torment and intimidation?_____

> "Father help us not to compare ourselves to others and make ridiculous standards, help us to be ourselves, in Jesus name!"

Day 30

.... What's your gift? .... I'm not officially anybody I just do what I want...

.... and my want is to encourage, ... that's my gift. The way I found that out was figuring what I like to do and go with it. When the church got the new building we were hoping for, we walked and prayed over the rooms, not forgetting even the bathrooms because I told them .... "thats my best place of ministry!" One of my favorite memories of stepping out on the gift of compassion was when I bowed my head as I entered the door of the church that Sunday, praying .... "Lord lead me to whom you want me to speak today." As I walked forward .... a women, sitting alone caught my eye and as I began speaking and sharing from my own struggles, I found myself begin to flow prophetically. My words were being an ointment to her heart. Normally I just try to generally be uplifting where ever I am but this time I was applying myself consciously and found God met me that day. Her husband happened to walk up exclaiming . . . . "how did you know that? It's exactly what she's going through!" . . . . walking away there were a lot of different emotions. Joy because it felt good to be used of the Lord, but a little regret that I hadn't stepped out more.

day 30 . . . . There are so many needs in a church, if we had X-ray eyes and could see into the lives of those that sat around us, how could we help?" _____

> "Father, please help us to be more prepared for the times we meet together as a whole body, help us to be more alert and not so self-absorbed, in Jesus name amen."

WITHDRAWN
SYRACUSE PUBLIC LIBRARY
Syracuse, Indiana